Motorbooks International

FARM TRACTOR COLOR HISTORY

MASSEY
TRACTORS

Text by C. H. Wendel
Photography by Andrew Morland

First published in 1992 by Motorbooks International Publishers & Wholesalers, PO Box 2, 729 Prospect Avenue, Osceola, WI 54020 USA

Motorbooks International books are also available at discounts in bulk quantity for industrial or sales-promotional use. For details write to Special Sales Manager at the Publisher's address

Library of Congress Cataloging-in-Publication Data
Wendel, C. H. (Charles H.)
    Massey tractors / C. H. Wendel, Andrew Morland.
        p.   cm.—(Motorbooks International farm tractor color history)
    Includes index.
    ISBN 0-87938-618-5
    1. Massey tractors—History.   2. Massey tractors—Pictorial works.
    I. Morland, Andrew.   II. Title.   III. Series.
    TL233.5.W45 1992
    629.225—dc20   92-18370
Printed and bound in Singapore by P.H Productions

On the front cover: The Massey-Harris 333 Row-Crop tractor was developed from the earlier 33 model. This model, owned by John Fisher of Milton, Ontario, was built in 1956.

On the frontispiece: The Massey-Harris 3 was powered by a four-cylinder Buda engine generating 15-28hp. This model was photographed on the grounds of the Ontario Agricultural Museum, which owns this tractor.

On the title page: The Massey-Harris Pony was a relatively small tractor used primarily for truck farming and other light work. The Pony model was built from 1948-1957.

On the back cover: The Massey-Harris Pacemaker was introduced in 1936 and was replaced after two years by the Streamlined Pacemaker; this model is owned by the Schmidt family of Bluffton, Ohio. Also a Massey-Harris Model 33 with a 33 Spring Tooth Cultivator.

Contents

Acknowledgments

The author wishes to extend a special thanks to Mr. Andrew Morland, who took the photographs used in this book. The catalog photos are from literature in the author's private collection. Although an in-depth history of the company would require far more material, this title is intended to give a pictorial overview of Massey-Harris and its related companies. Should the reader find any errors, and there probably are some, please direct your correspondence to the author in care of Motorbooks International.

C. H. Wendel

Thanks to all of the Massey-Harris tractor owners and enthusiasts whose help and cooperation made this book possible. Special thanks to the following people for letting me photograph their tractors: Sherwood Hume, David Stirk, the Schmidt family, Vic Lauer, Ivan Henderson, the Fisher family, Barry Tuck, the Reichert family, Fred Farms, Bill Kuhn, and Harry Bowen.

A very special thanks to the Ontario Agricultural Museum, Milton, Ontario, Canada, for letting me photograph their rare Massey No. 2 and No. 3 and GP 4WD on the grounds of their impressive museum. Their annual Great Canadian Antique Tractor Farm Field Days is a must for Massey enthusiasts.

Thanks also to the Old Time Threshing and Antique Engine Show at the Stephenson County Fairgrounds, Freeport, Illinois, and to the Great Dorset Steam Fair, Blandford, Great Britain. The British Massey photos were taken at their annual event at the end of August.

Andrew Morland

Introduction

From simple beginnings in 1847, Massey-Ferguson grew to be the largest farm tractor organization in the Western world. This came about largely because the Massey company began looking at overseas markets as early as the late 1860s. The high ranking of Massey implements at the 1867 International Exposition in Paris added tremendous impetus to a company that was already growing very rapidly. As the decades passed, Massey Manufacturing Company and A. Harris, Son & Company joined forces, and the M-H combination succeeded in making numerous important acquisitions.

Many people associate the Massey-Harris name with the self-propelled combine. When the M-H-20 appeared in 1938, it was indeed the world's first self-propelled combine. Within a few decades, this machine revolutionized the grain harvest in most parts of the world. Not only did the self-propelled combine sound the death knell for the grain binder, the thresher, and its heavy labor requirements, it also brought an end to small combines operated by tractor power. Granted, there were other companies also entering the market and numerous combine developments would emerge from competing companies. But the simple fact remains that it was Massey-Harris that was responsible for developing this unprecedented machine.

In its early years, Massey-Harris concentrated heavily on harvesting equipment, including mowers and grain binders. The company also built an extensive line of primary and secondary tillage implements.

Entering the farm tractor business presented numerous obstacles for Massey-Harris, some of which came as expensive lessons. The initial entry was made with the Big Bull tractor, at a time when the Big Bull was falling out of favor with the farmer. No disrespect intended, but this particular design hit the market like a prairie fire. After a few short years, farmers were looking for something better in a small tractor, and the Big Bull left the market just as quickly as it entered.

The company's second tractor venture was to obtain manufacturing rights for the Parrett tractor, manufactured by Parrett Tractor Company of Chicago, Illinois, which had gained some respectable press in the United States. M-H built a plant in Weston, Ontario, for tractor production, but the Parrett was yet another design destined for failure. The design was rather attractive, and the tractor was well built, but from 1910 to 1925 farm tractor styles were changing rapidly. In fact, the evolution of the tractor was so rapid that designs were often obsolete before production even began, and some were obsolete before getting to the drawing board.

Not until Massey-Harris bought out the J. I. Case Plow Works did it seriously enter the tractor business. This time the company had a proven design and an established dealer organization. The rest is history. Beginning with the Wallis models, and continuing on through the Challenger, Pacemaker, and other tractors, the Massey-Harris tractor line continued without interruption. Merging with Harry Ferguson Incorporated put yet another feather in the company's cap, and Massey-Ferguson tractors today are marketed throughout the world.

In working within the format of this book it has been impossible to include many desirable photographs, illustrations, and much historical information. Thus, we have frequently cited other titles in which this information may be found. They include *150 Years of J. I. Case, Nebraska Tractor Tests since 1920,* and *Encyclopedia of American Farm Tractors,* all by C. H. Wendel.

As far as we know, dates given are reasonably correct, although the available industry guides and even the company's own product information sometimes is not in agreement. Should readers note any errors or discrepancies, please notify us through the publisher. It should also be noted that our commentary regarding the various machines described herein is our own opinion, and is intended to neither add to nor subtract from the efficacy of Massey-Harris or Massey-Ferguson products. Our sole aim is to preserve in print some of the highlights of a most interesting company as seen through its products.

C. H. Wendel
April 15, 1992

A pair of very rare Sawyer-Massey
tractors built in 1921. Both are 20-40
models built by the Sawyer-Massey
Company at Hamilton, Ontario. This
firm operated with financial backing
from the Massey family. The two
tractors shown here were photographed
at the Great Canadian Antique Tractor
Farm Field Days held at the Ontario
Agricultural Museum.

Chapter 1

Massey-Harris Limited

Daniel Massey was a farmer. In 1847 he began manufacturing simple implements at Newcastle, Ontario. He was so successful that farming soon became secondary to the manufacturing business.

A decade later, Alanson Harris began building farm implements, eventually settling in Brantford, Ontario, Canada. Massey Manufacturing Company moved from Newcastle to Toronto in 1879.

Along with building implements tailored specifically for the Canadian farmer, Massey also secured manufacturing rights for numerous implements that were being developed in the United States. Included were the Wood self-rake reaper and the Ketchum mower. Walter A. Wood's mower appeared in the Massey catalog of 1862. In 1881, Massey acquired the Toronto Reaper & Mower Company. Then in 1875, Massey purchased the patents for Sharp's dump rake. It was so successful that five years later, the company sold over 3,000 of these implements.

The open-end grain binder developed by the A. Harris, Son & Company in 1891 was an instantaneous success. In fact, it was this machine that prodded Massey and Harris into an 1891 merger. Almost immediately after the merger, Massey-Harris bought out the Patterson-Wisner Company which was itself a merger of two major plow builders. Then came the buyout of the Verity Plow Company at Exeter, Ontario. Two years after the merger, Massey-Harris bought out the Corbin Disc

Harrow Company of Prescott, Ontario. The Bain Wagon Company of Woodstock, Ontario, came into the fold during 1895. Sometime in 1904 the company bought the Kemp Manure Spreader Company at Stratford, Ontario. Then in 1910, it bought out Deyo-Macey Engine Company at Binghamton, New York. The plant was moved to the new Massey-Harris factory at Weston, Ontario, and Massey-Harris engines began emerging that same year.

During these years the Massey-Harris firm grew steadily. The company was constantly diversifying, and had achieved status as a major farm equipment manufacturer. In 1910 Massey-Harris acquired its first factory outside of Canada. This happened with the purchase of a controlling interest in the Johnston Harvester Company of Batavia, New York. M-H bought the Johnston factories largely because of fears that the 1910 Reciprocity Act might become law. The fear was that this law might flood the Canadian market with imports from south of the border. Johnston also had an extensive export trade, and Massey-Harris was already a major exporter of farm implements.

In 1917 Massey-Harris entered the tractor market. Initially the Bull tractor, which had had a brief heyday in the United States, was the tractor of choice. However, it was no more successful in Canada than it had been in the United States. During 1919 the company began building Parrett tractors at its Weston plant. These were sold as No. 1, No. 2, and

A Sawyer-Massey 20-40 tractor of 1921 vintage. All Sawyer-Massey models of the period carried four-cylinder engines. Sawyer-Massey began building tractors in 1910, with production of this style continuing into the early 1920s. This model carried an engine using a $5^5/8$x7in bore and stroke. The valve-in-head design was rated at only 340rpm.

In 1918 the Sawyer-Massey 20-40 tractor listed at $3,750. That year, Sawyer-Massey offered four models: the 11-22, the 17-34, the 20-40, and the big 27-50 model. The latter carried a four-cylinder engine having a $6^1/4$x8in bore and stroke. It weighed 17,500lb, and listed at $4,000. The three largest models used a Bennett carburetor; the 11-22 tractor featured a Kingston carburetor.

Sawyer-Massey began building portable steam engines in the 1860s. When this 22-68 steamer was built in 1919, the Sawyer-Massey Co. had become one of the largest steam traction engine builders in the world. Sawyer-Massey had roots going back to 1836. In that same year John Fisher built his first thresher. Later on, John Sawyer went to work for Fisher, buying out the company in 1856. The Massey family purchased 40 percent of the Sawyer Company in 1892, renaming the firm Sawyer-Massey.

No. 3 models, each reflecting various modifications to the design. Production ceased in 1923, however.

Although part of the Parrett tractor's meager success was likely due to the tractor itself, there were mitigating factors as well. For one thing, the Canadian tariff on tractors selling for under $1,400 was completely removed. This raised the competition level to frenzied heights. It is also possible that the marketing strategy for the M-H models might not have

been designed as effectively as it should have been.

Already in 1926, Massey-Harris began negotiating with J. I. Case Plow Works at Racine, Wisconsin, for Canadian marketing rights to their Wallis tractor. Case Plow Works made overtures to buy out the M-H shares held by the Massey foundation and the Massey family. A syndicate was quickly formed which bought out the Massey interests, and from

that point on, the Massey family no longer controlled the company.

With the Massey family now outside the realm, negotiations with the Plow Works continued, and in 1927 M-H obtained sales rights for the Wallis Certified both in Canada and in certain parts of the United States. The following year it bought out the Plow Works for $1.3 million in cash, plus the guarantee of $1.1 million in outstanding bonds. Massey-Harris immediately sold all rights to the "Case" name back to the J. I. Case Threshing Machine Company, also of Racine, Wisconsin. The use of the Case name had been a matter of controversy for some years between the Threshing Machine

Company and the Plow Works. (For further information in this regard, as well as manufacturing activities of the Plow Works, refer to *150 Years of J. I. Case* by C. H. Wendel.)

Massey-Harris established a dominant role in the foreign markets early in its history. For example, Cie Massey-Harris S.A. was established in France in 1927. It replaced an earlier firm that had been building Johnston harvesting equipment in France for some years. Massey-Harris GmbH was established in Germany in 1902. Massey grain binders found their way to Australia in the early 1880s. Eventually this operation was amalgamated into H. V. McKay–Massey-Harris Proprietary Limited.

In 1912 the Wallis Tractor Company built a total of nine Wallis Bear tractors. Shown here is the third one of the lot, and the only one known to exist. It carries Serial No. 203. The massive engine has a displacement of 1480ci (cubic inches). Total weight of this tractor is 10½ tons. Despite its weight, the Wallis Bear was somewhat ahead of its time.

Massey-Harris-Ferguson acquired this firm in 1955.

Tom Carroll, an Australian-born Massey-Harris engineer, was largely responsible for the 1938 introduction of the M-H self-propelled combine. The M-H Harvest Brigade eventually

• WALLIS BEAR •

THIS TRACTOR WAS BUILT BEFORE 1912, BEING THE THIRD
ONE MADE OUT OF A TOTAL OF NINE AND IS THE ONLY ONE
LEFT IN EXISTENCE TODAY. THIS TRACTOR HAS POWER STEER-
ING, INDIVIDUAL TURNING BRAKES, SPRING LOADED CLUTCH,
ENCLOSED 3-SPEED TRANSMISSION, ALLSPEED GOVERNOR,
GASOLINE MOTOR HAS 7½ INCH BORE AND 9 INCH STROKE
(1400 CUBIC INCH DISPLACEMENT), GEAR OIL PUMP WITH FORCE
FEED TO CONNECTING RODS AND WRIST PINS, REAR DRIVE
WHEELS ARE 7 FEET IN DIAMETER WITH 30 INCH FACE, WEIGHS
15 1/2 TON, WAS DESIGNED TO PULL 8 TO 10 PLOW BOTTOMS.

OWNERS ◄   SCHMIDT MACHINE CO.
        OFFICE SAN JOSE, OHIO
        E. F. S.

A rear view of the Wallis Bear illustrates the rear-mounted belt pulley. H. M. Wallis, founder of the company, was a son-in-law of J. I. Case. After Case's death in 1891, Wallis headed up the J. I. Case Plow Works, an entirely separate entity from the J. I. Case Threshing Machine Co. The Wallis tractors were built in the shops of the Plow Works, and in about 1918 the Wallis Tractor Co. name was dropped in favor of the Plow Works title.

revolutionized harvesting methods throughout the world.

One of the more notable mergers of recent times came in 1953 when Harry Ferguson Inc. and Massey-Harris Ltd. agreed to combine forces. The Ferguson system integrated the tractor and the implement. With Harry Ferguson's three-point design, the bottom links pulled the implement forward. The top link trans-ferred force applied by the implement into a forward pressure. The effect was to add weight, and traction, to the rear wheels of the tractor.

Harry Ferguson and Henry Ford had made an oral agreement in 1938, whereby Ford would produce the Ferguson tractor. All went well for a time, but eventually Ferguson filed suit against Ford, receiving $9.25 million as a settlement with respect to patent royalties. After breaking with Ford, the Ferguson team built a complete factory and produced their

This photograph shows the massive fenders used on the Wallis Bear, along with the large fuel tanks necessary for the huge engine. It has been said that the Wallis Bear was somehow connected with the earlier development of another huge tractor built between 1912 and 1914 by the Ajax Auto Traction Company at Portland, Oregon.

• WALLIS BEAR

THIS TRACTOR WAS BUILT BEFORE 1912, BEING THE
THIRD ONE MADE OUT OF A TOTAL OF NINE AND IS THE
ONLY ONE LEFT IN EXISTENCE TODAY. THIS TRACTOR
HAS POWER STEERING, INDIVIDUAL TURNING BRAKES,
SPRING LOADED CLUTCH, ENCLOSED 3-SPEED TRANSMISS-
ION, ALL SPEED GOVERNOR, GASOLINE MOTOR HAS 7½ INCH BORE
AND 9 INCH STROKE (1480 CUBIC INCH DISPLACEMENT), GEAR OIL
PUMP WITH FORCE FEED TO CONNECTING RODS AND WRIST PINS,
REAR DRIVE WHEELS ARE 7 FEET IN DIAMETER WITH 30 INCH FACES
WEIGHT IS 10½ TON WAS DESIGNED TO PULL 8 TO 10 PLOW BOTTOMS

OWNERS ← SCHMIDT MACHINE CO.
UPPER SANDUSKY, OHIO.

E.F. SCHMIDT et
BLUFFTON, OHIO.

WALLIS BEAR

THIS TRACTOR WAS BUILT BEFORE 1912, BEING THE THIRD
ONE, MADE OUT OF A TOTAL OF NINE AND IS THE ONLY ONE
LEFT IN EXISTENCE TODAY. THIS TRACTOR HAS POWER STEER-
ING, INDIVIDUAL TURNING BRAKES, SPRING LOADED CLUTCH,
ENCLOSED 3-SPEED TRANSMISSION, ALLSPEED GOVERNOR,
GASOLINE MOTOR HAS 7½ INCH BORE AND 9 INCH STROKE
(480 CUBIC INCH DISPLACEMENT), GEAR OIL PUMP WITH FORCE
CONNECTING RODS AND WRIST PINS, GEAR DRIVE,

Previous page
E. F. Schmidt of Bluffton, Ohio, stands by one of the 7ft drivers on his Wallis Bear tractor. Schmidt was a Massey-Harris dealer for many years. Even though the Wallis Bear can hardly be considered a successful production model, it nevertheless paved the way for a series of Wallis tractors that proved to be trendsetters in the industry.

E. F. Schmidt's son with crank in hand, ready to start the engine. A shaft ran through the transmission from the rear of the tractor to the back of the engine crankshaft. All reports are that the Bear started easily. This would have been expedient, since cranking an engine of this size for any length of time was beyond the physical capabilities of any person.

first Ferguson tractor on October 11, 1948.

On October 31, 1953, Massey-Harris and Ferguson joined forces with a new company known as Massey-Harris-Ferguson Limited. In March 1958 the name was abbreviated to Massey-Ferguson Limited. (See chapter 3.)

Other interesting Massey acquisitions along the way include the Perkins Diesel Engine Company in 1959. Founded by Frank Perkins in 1932, the company had grown into one of the world's major builders of diesel engines. In 1966 the company acquired an interest in Motor Iberica, a major Spanish producer of tractors and trucks.

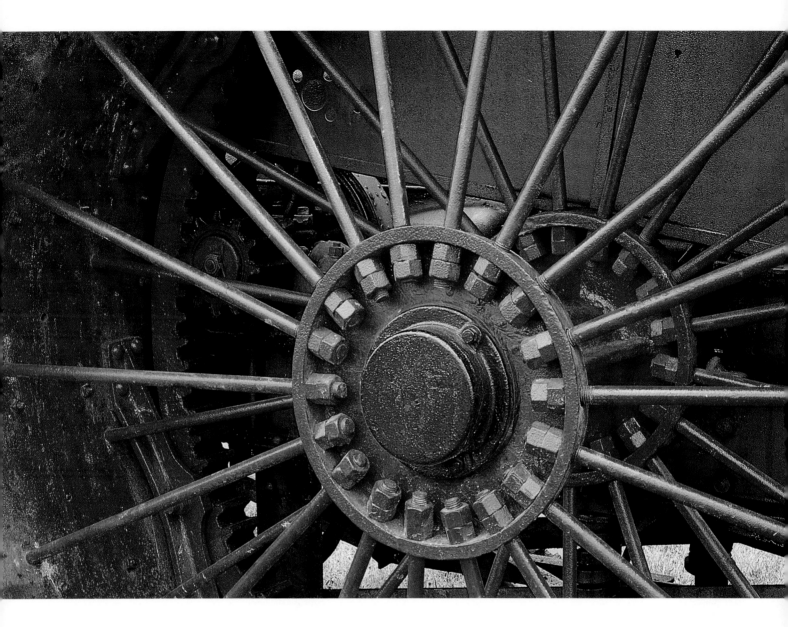

Wallis Bear tractors used a 7ft drivewheel with a 30in face. Even with drivers of this size, ground pressure was considerable, due to the machine's total weight of more than 20,000lb. As was the case with all tractors of this period, the bull gears and pinions operated in open air and were exposed to every sort of dirt and grit. Two schools of thought prevailed. One was that the bull gears should be heavily lubricated to enhance their usefulness. The other theory was that lubricants did little more than bond the gritty material to the gear teeth. Therefore, it was reasoned, it was better to leave the gears dry, with no lubricant whatsoever.

The Sawyer-Massey Co. in Canada had no connection with J. I. Case Plow Works of Wisconsin. Actually, in 1892 the Massey family had joined with the company formed by Alanson Harris thirty-five years earlier. Massey-Harris sold various tractor models after 1910, but never had a tractor they could call their own. This did not happen until M-H bought out the J. I. Case Plow Works in 1927. The convoluted history of the Sawyer, Massey, and Harris companies brought more and more manufacturing entities together, but their primary emphasis was on implement lines. By the purchase of the Plow Works in 1927, M-H was able to enter the US tractor market as a major contender. Shown is a view of the gigantic engine used in the Wallis Bear.

A huge radiator was needed for the Wallis Bear, and it was placed at the extreme front of the tractor. Due to the front wheels being obstructed from view, a directional arrow was mounted on a vertical shaft, and clearly within view of the operator. This tractor offered numerous forward features, including power steering, separate turning brakes, and a spring-loaded clutch.

Although Sawyer-Massey had been in the tractor business since 1910, the Massey-Harris Co. did not enter the tractor trade until 1917. That year the company entered the Canadian tractor market with the Big Bull tractor, built by Bull Tractor Company of Minneapolis, Minnesota. The Massey-Harris No. 1 tractor came out the following year, built at the Weston works on the outskirts of Toronto. A few months later, slight modifications resulted in the M-H No. 2 model. The M-H No. 2 shown here is of 1921 vintage.

The Big Bull—$585
F. O. B. Minneapolis, Minn.

Over 7,000 Bull Tractors Working on American Farms

Exclusive Features of the BIG BULL

1. The Bull Wheel runs in the furrow and does not pack the land. This principle is covered by patent.

2. The patent *Steer Wheel*, also running in the furrow in line with the bull wheel, makes the tractor positively and automatically self-steering.

3. Patent leveling device by which the tractor is quickly and easily adjusted to side hills or deep furrows.

4. Direct drive with only four gears. All complicated transmission and compensating gears absolutely eliminated.

5. Special gear-shifting device.

6. Electric welded gasoline tank and brass tube radiator.

7. Extra large crank shaft and connecting rod bearings.

8. Extra large inspection plate on top of motor, affording easy examination of bearings without disturbing timing.

MOTOR

10 H. P. at drawbar; 7 guaranteed. 25 H. P. at belt; 20 guaranteed. The motor is the best and most practical power plant ever produced for small tractors.

Lubrication—we use the Detroit Lubricator—having 500 lbs. pressure per square inch—also splash system.

Ignition—Choice between Kingston or Sevison Magnetos.

Carburetor—Kingston.

THE BULL TRACTOR CO.   Minneapolis, Minn.

Massey-Harris attempted to enter the gas tractor market by marketing its Bull tractor. The Bull took the industry by storm, since it was one of the first "small" tractors. Farmers were crying for a small tractor, as compared to the huge OilPull, the Twin City, and others that had tremendous power, but were huge in size and enormously expensive to buy and operate. Massey-Harris sold the Big Bull in Canada during 1917. However, "disappointing" is the term that best describes its success.

Massey-Harris built the Parrett design through a license agreement with the Parrett Tractor Co. of Chicago, Illinois. This model was designed by Dent and Henry Parrett. It was sold on the American market for several years. Parrett Tractor was originally based in Ottawa, Illinois, and eventually moved to Chicago. Dent Parrett was also involved with building motorized cultivators. He appears again in the 1930s with a company known as Parrett Tractors of Benton Harbor, Michigan.

The Parrett Model D tractor was tested at Nebraska in 1920. The American version carried a Buda four-cylinder engine with a rating of 15 drawbar and 30 belt hp. In fact, the Model D was tested at Nebraska's Tractor Test Laboratory in 1920 under No. 37. In the book *A Global Corporation*, E. P. Neufeld states regarding the No. 2 tractor that "[The] attempt to build tractors at the Weston plant from 1919 to 1923 was a failure, and not till 1927 did it begin distribution of the 20-30 Wallis Certified Tractor."

Massey-Harris No. 2 tractors carried a Buda four-cylinder engine having a $4\frac{1}{4}$x$5\frac{1}{2}$in bore and stroke. Weighing 5,200lb, it carried a 1918 list price of $1,450. This closeup view shows the timing gear case and the uncommon radiator placement.

A closeup view of the operator's platform, which perpetually asks the operator, "Did you oil up?" A Madison-Kipp force-feed lubricator was used for the engine, and it required regular replenishment to ensure proper lubrication. In addition, virtually every bearing was furnished with an oil reservoir and a grease cup. Depending on various factors, some bearings needed lubrication every couple of hours, while others needed refilling only once or twice a day.

The Massey-Harris No. 3 was the immediate successor to the No. 2, and it reflected the increased horsepower rating to 15 drawbar and 28 belt hp. This change apparently resulted from raising the cylinder bore from $4^{1}/_{4}$ to $4^{1}/_{2}$in. Despite glowing claims by the company, sales of the Massey-built Parrett tractors were less than enormous, and in 1923, production of the M-H No. 3 ended at the Weston plant. On the US side of the border, Parrett succumbed to the postwar depression and intense competition. The company disappeared from the industry about 1922. The tractor pictured is owned by the Ontario Agricultural Museum.

Another Massey-Harris No. 2 that has been restored. This one is finished in a brighter shade of red than the one owned by the Ontario Agricultural Museum, but both are thought to be original colors. The rubber tread on this tractor is, of course, not original; it does, however, permit the tractor to be used on paved streets for parades and the like.

The Ontario Agricultural Museum owns this Massey-Harris No. 3 tractor. As noted elsewhere, the No. 3 was a last-ditch effort to save the design, ostensibly by increasing the horsepower. The effort failed, however; farmers simply weren't buying many tractors during the early 1920s, due to a financial depression following World War I. Many farmers lost all they had, and others who didn't go broke were severely set back. By the time recovery began in the mid-1920s, the talk of a row-crop tractor was in the air, so tractors like the M-H No. 3 found little market.

A closeup view of the powerplant used on the No. 3 model illustrates the unique belt drive for the cooling fan. It was driven from the cam gear train, with a belt running between the fan and the drive pulley. It is ironic that flat belts were the accepted practice for many years. With the development of reliable V-belt drives, the flat belt virtually left the scene. Recent years have witnessed the rebirth of an improved flat-belt design in modern automotive practice.

Moving the radiator from its former position to that shown here was an obvious change on the Massey-Harris No. 3. By placing the radiator crosswise of the frame, the tractor took on an entirely different appearance. This was complicated by the fact that the Parrett design used exceptionally large front wheels, and they required a lot of clearance when turning.

A view from the operator's platform illustrates its general arrangement. Although the heat of the engine made this a very hot place in summer, it was rather cozy during the cold months of winter. During its production run, Massey-Harris changed the gear ratios several times, in order to get what they thought was the correct combination of the two available forward speeds. While earlier models had speeds of 2½ and 4mph, the later models lowered these figures to 1¾ and 2½mph.

Wallis Model K tractors were built by the J. I. Case Plow Works at Racine, Wisconsin. As previously noted, this firm had no connection whatsoever with the J. I. Case Threshing Machine Co., also of Racine. The name similarity came from the fact that J. I. Case had founded both companies. After his death, the estate divested itself of all interest in the Threshing Machine Co., but continued with the J. I. Case Plow Works.

The Wallis Model K appeared in 1919. This model even included an air cleaner stack. While the original Wallis Cub used a fully enclosed transmission and open bull gears, this was changed in 1915 when the Model J, the Cub Junior, appeared. The Model K was the first tractor with a fully enclosed drivetrain, despite the claims of Henry Ford to be the first with a totally enclosed design. The Canadian Fairbanks-Morse Company began selling Wallis tractors in Canada in 1918.

This Wallis Model K is owned by Vic Lauer of Mount Union, Iowa. Model K tractors used the unit frame design that had been pioneered by Wallis Tractor Co. in 1913. US Patent No. 1,205,982 was issued to Clarence M. Eason and Robert O. Hendrickson in November 1913. The patent was assigned to the Wallis Tractor Co. Henry Ford claimed his Fordson to be the first unit frame tractor, but the Wallis preceded the Fordson design by several years. While Wallis used a boilerplate frame, the Fordson frame was an iron casting.

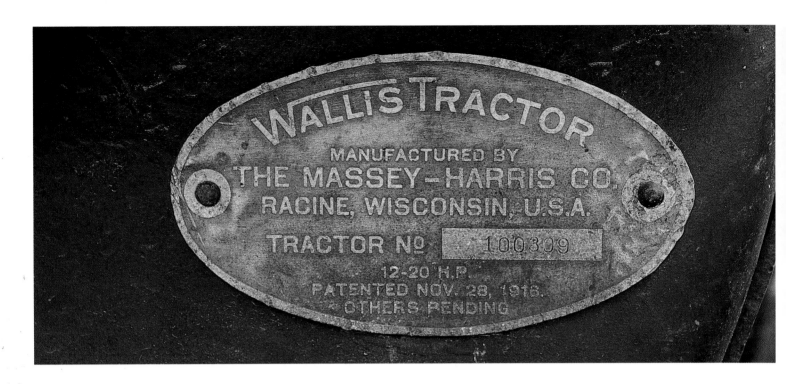

Massey-Harris introduced the 12-20 Wallis tractor in 1929, and it remained in production until 1934. Shown here is a 12-20 Wallis bearing Serial No. 100309. M-H bought out J. I. Case Plow Works in 1927, providing them with a fully equipped tractor factory. After paying $1.3 million for the company, M-H sold all rights to the Case name to J. I. Case Threshing Machine Co. for $700,000. In effect, Massey-Harris bought an established and reputable tractor company, complete with manufacturing facilities, for only $600,000.

Massey-Harris sold the Wallis tractors to a wide US and Canadian market. The company also sold them extensively through their international network of warehouses and dealerships. In fact, Massey-Harris was one of the leading multinational tractor and implement manufacturers of the 1930s. Of course, the Wallis tractor was named for H. M. Wallis, president of J. I. Case Plow Works. Wallis was a son-in-law of J. I. Case.

In Nebraska Test No. 164 of 1929 the Wallis 12-20 delivered slightly over 24 belt hp burning distillate fuel. Like its predecessors, this tractor was equipped with the company's own four-cylinder engine. In this instance, the engine was rated at 1000rpm and had a $3^7/_8$x$5^1/_4$in bore and stroke. The engine block was bolted directly to the boilerplate frame, with the frame serving as the crankcase. Handhole plates in the steel frame provided access to the connecting rod bearings.

WALLIS AIR CLEANER
WARRANTY DOES NOT APPLY UNLESS THESE INSTRUCTIONS ARE FOLLOWED
1. DRAIN AND REFILL CLEANER WITH USED CRANK CASE OIL TO TOP OF FILLER OPENING.
2. DRAIN AND REFILL AT LEAST TWICE A WEEK OR OFTEN ENOUGH TO PREVENT DUST FILLING MORE THAN ¼ INCH DEEP IN OIL CHAMBER OR NOZZLE CHAMBER.
4. WHEN YOU DRAIN, ALWAYS REMOVE BOTTOM PLATE AND SCRAPE DIRT AND SETTLINGS FROM BOTTOM OF OIL CHAMBER AND NOZZLE CHAMBER AND SIDES OF VERTICAL NOZZLE CHAMBER.
5. LOCATE AND CLEAN OIL FEED NOZZLE WITH A WIRE.

PATENTED MARCH 23, 1926

The New....
MASSEY-HARRIS
MODEL 25

The Massey-Harris Model 25 tractor appeared about 1933. It replaced the earlier 20-30 model. Apparently, the MH-25 remained available up to 1940, the last year for which pricing information has been located. In that year the 25 on steel wheels had a retail price of $1,275. If furnished on rubber tires, the price was $1,530. Standard equipment included 12³/₄x28in tires. On steel wheels, the Model 25 weighed 5,000lb, and 500lb less when furnished with rubber tires.

Previous page
Many tractors of the early 1930s burned kerosene or distillate. This required an air preheater or some other preheating means for the intake air. Industry jargon often refers to this as a "hot" manifold. Shown here is the air cleaner and preheater system used on the Wallis 12-20 and other Wallis models of the period.

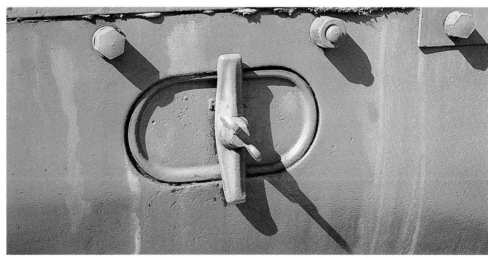

Handhole plates similar in appearance to those used on steam traction engines were the only access to the interior of the crankcase. Despite the fact that today's modern lubricants were then only a dream, very little service work was required. With reasonable care and regular oil changes, these engines would run for years with little attention required for the bottom of the engine. Problems with leaking, worn, or burnt valves were far more prevalent.

THE LAST WORD IN TRACTOR DESIGN

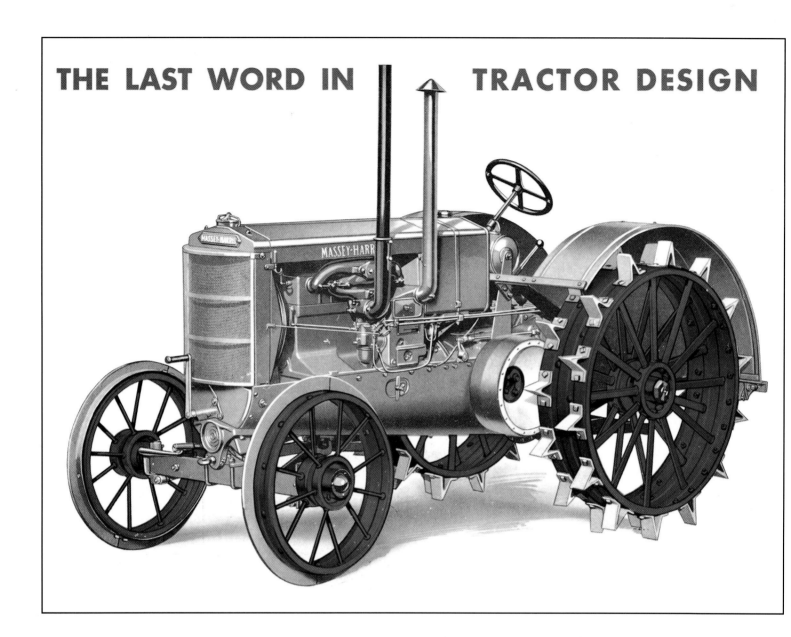

This view illustrates the location of the belt pulley for the Model 25. In fact, the belt pulley assumed this location for several earlier models. Model 25 tractors were essentially the same as the earlier 20-30 Wallis. A notable change, however, was that the 25 had an engine speed of 1200rpm, while the earlier 20-30 tractor operated at 1050rpm. Nebraska Test No. 134 covers the 20-30, and Test No. 219 applies to the Model 25.

Next page
A rear view of the Model 25 shows the optional power takeoff shaft. At this time, these shaft sizes and locations were not standardized, making it necessary to buy the coupling and shaft equipment for adaptation to a specific implement. (Further details concerning the Wallis tractors may be found in the book, *150 Years of J. I. Case* by C. H. Wendel.)

Numerous implements were available for the Massey-Harris General Purpose tractor. Despite this, sales of the four-wheel-drive design were not at all sensational. Competitors like Allis-Chalmers were concurrently developing lightweight row-crop designs, and the latter was also developing tractors with pneumatic tires. The G-P tractor also had its own unique hazards. Trying to back up while headed downhill, or backing out of a ditch, could be hazardous, since the back of the tractor tended to rear up under these conditions.

Previous page
Announced in 1930, the Massey-Harris General Purpose (G-P) tractor was the first tractor designed from within the company. The four-wheel-drive design was technically advanced, although it was not the first tractor built with this general design. Four-wheel-drive designs are accepted practice today, along with front-wheel-assist drive systems. As with the earlier Wallis tractor designs, this tractor was likewise ahead of its time.

The General Purpose model was equipped with a Hercules four-cylinder, 226ci engine. Its four cylinders used a 4x4½in bore and stroke with a rated speed of 1200rpm. Standard equipment included a Zenith carburetor and an American Bosch U-4 magneto. This model was tested at Nebraska in 1930 under Test No. 177. It was tested again the following year, this time under No. 191. The only difference was that in the first test, gasoline fuel was used, while in the latter test, distillate was the fuel of choice. This Massey-Harris G-P is owned by the Ontario Agricultural Museum.

This closeup view of a Massey-Harris General Purpose tractor illustrates its Hercules powerplant. The G-P was an entirely new design for Massey-Harris— it did not follow the designs used in the Wallis tractor line at all. Thus, the Wallis engines would not work with this tractor. In fact, adapting these engines to the G-P would have been nearly impossible, since the Wallis engines had no self-contained crankcase. It was formed by the boiler-plate frame of the tractor. So, Massey-Harris used a four-cylinder Hercules engine for this model.

The Massey-Harris Pacemaker was
introduced in 1936 and was also built
the following year. Rated at 16 drawbar
and 27 belt hp, this design was a takeoff
from the earlier 12-20 tractor. A four-
speed transmission was used. This
surviving copy is owned by the Schmidt
family of Bluffton, Ohio.

A closeup of the Schmidts' Pacemaker tractor illustrates the unique manifold system. This was necessary for burning distillate or other low-grade fuels. Since kerosene and distillate were less expensive than gasoline, their use remained popular for some years. However, the additional service problems caused by crankcase dilution and carbon deposits were a disadvantage. These fuels were also unable to squeeze out as much power as gasoline fuel.

Nebraska Test No. 266 of August 1936 covers the Massey-Harris Pacemaker. This standard-tread tractor carried a four-cylinder engine having a $3^{7}/_{8}$x$5^{1}/_{4}$in bore and stroke. The previous test, No. 265, was for the M-H Challenger, a row-crop tractor that carried the same four-cylinder engine as the Pacemaker. The Pacemaker was built through 1937, and the following year it was replaced with the streamlined Pacemaker model.

Massey-Harris Challenger tractors were row-crop tractors developed from the earlier 12-20 Wallis, the latter being a standard-tread model. The Challenger followed the same general lines as the earlier Wallis tractors, complete with the boilerplate frame. Challenger tractors used the company's own four-cylinder engine with a 3⁷/₈x5¹/₄in bore and stroke. It was rated at 1200rpm, and was capable of about 26 belt hp.

The Massey-Harris Challenger was tested at Nebraska in 1936. In this test it burned distillate fuel. During a drawbar test it pulled 2,883lb, or about 69 percent of its 4,200lb operating weight. Its forerunner, the Wallis 12-20, had been tested at Nebraska in 1929 but carried a rated speed of only 1000rpm. However, the gutsy little 12-20 pulled nearly 78 percent of its 3,900lb operating weight in Test No. 164.

Diane Fisher of Hamilton, Ontario, owns this 1942 Massey-Harris Model 81-R tractor. The Model 81 saw extensive use by the Royal Canadian Air Force during World War II for towing aircraft. These tractors were not painted red, but were finished in the usual camouflage colors. The Model 81 standard-tread was built from 1941 to 1946; production on the Model 81 row-crop style began the same year, ending in 1948. However, no Model 81 tractors were built in 1943, and the Model 81 row-crop version was not built in 1946–47.

Previous page
Owned by the Reichert family of Ilderton, Ontario, this M-H Challenger was built in 1938. Challenger models could be furnished with steel wheels or rubber tires, at the option of the original purchaser. On rubber, it had an operating weight of 3,915lb. When equipped with steel wheels, it sold for $995. Buying it with 10-36 rubber tires raised the price to $1,205. Here's owner Reichert at the controls. Photographed at the Ontario Agricultural Museum.

Model 81 standard-tread tractors were available from 1941 to 1946. It appears that they were also available in the 1947 model year. The 81 carried a Continental four-cylinder engine with a 3x4³/₈in bore and stroke, for a displacement of 124ci. Apparently, this model was available only on 9x32in rubber tires. Thus equipped, it retailed at $811. The 81 also featured Twin-Power, which amounted to nothing more than two different engine speeds.

Totally original, this Massey-Harris 101 Super Standard tractor was built in 1939. It is owned by the Reichert family. When purchased with steel wheels, the tractor sold for about $1,400, but with rubber tires, as shown here, it retailed for about $1,750. The 101 featured a Chrysler T57-503 engine, and servicing was available through the M-H dealer network, or from Chrysler dealers. The 101 Super Standard was also known as the Twin-Power 101 Standard.

Massey-Harris Model 81 row-crop tractors were offered during the same 1941—46 period as the Model 81 standard-tread. Except for the different front axle, the two tractors were essentially the same. Massey-Harris advertised the row-crop model as a two-plow tractor, making it ideal for a two-row cultivator. In fact, M-H offered an extensive line of cultivators to suit virtually any crop requirement. In 1945 the Model 81 row-crop retailed at $1,121. It was tested at Nebraska, with the results appearing in No. 376.

A closeup of the hood on Reichert's 101 Super Standard also illustrates the Twin-Power decal. Incredibly, this 1939 model is completely original, and is used on a regular basis by the Reichert family. At this writing, the 101 Super Standard pictured is more than fifty years old. One can't help but wonder how many of today's tractors will make it to the half-century mark!

Previous page
Massey-Harris sent a copy of their 101 Super Standard to Nebraska in September 1938. The six-cylinder engine carried a $3^{1}/_{8}$x$4^{3}/_{8}$in bore and stroke and was rated at 1500rpm on the drawbar and 1800rpm for belt work. As previously indicated, this was the sum and substance of the Twin-Power feature; all it consisted of was raising the engine speed by 300rpm. Production of this model ran from 1938 to 1946.

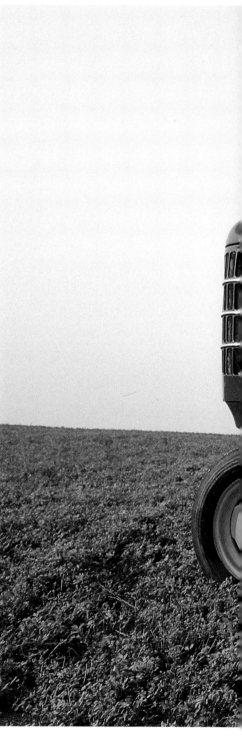

The 101 Super Standard was tested at Nebraska (Test No. 306) at the two different engine speeds needed for the Twin-Power feature. It was also tested on steel wheels and on rubber tires. Standard features of this model included an Auto-Lite electrical system with electric starting, but numerous others still had to be started by hand, either using a crank or by twisting a flywheel.

Scott Fred of Fred Farms in Indiana owns this nicely restored 1941 101 Super Row-Crop model. Like the Super Standard, this model was built from 1938 to 1946. Nebraska Test No. 307 of 1938 notes that the 101 Row-Crop model was tested both on steel wheels and on rubber tires. This was necessary because of the entirely different drawbar statistics that resulted. Despite the popularity of rubber tires, a substantial number of farmers still chose steel wheels. In perspective, choosing rubber tires was a major decision, since less than a decade earlier, most field work was done either with horses or with a heavy standard-tread tractor.

Harry Bowen of Orangeville, Illinois, owns this 101 Super Row-Crop model. Built in 1939, the streamlined styling was typical of the period, but the 101 had an appearance that was distinctive, with definite leanings toward automotive designs. The vented side panels were attractive, but impaired airflow over the engine. Thus, a great many of the side panels disappeared when overheating became a problem. Some collectors claim that this 101 Super model is the most collectible of the early Massey-Harris tractors.

A front view of Harry Bowen's 101 Super Row-Crop model illustrates the highly streamlined hood design. As an interesting sidelight, several of the major builders opted for a streamlined design in 1937 and 1938. Gone was the open fuel tank, the open radiator, and the open steering gear. While the early 1930s were years of practicality, the latter part of the decade saw cosmetic changes that essentially did nothing more than make the tractor more attractive.

Massey-Harris, and for that matter, all competing companies, did their best to make their tractors as appealing as possible. This included the use of bright colors such as red, green, and orange. In addition, decals were strategically located to not only serve as a model designator, but also to enhance the body finish. No doubt, a great deal of time was spent in deciding on the design of the decals so they would deliver maximum impact.

Next page
A platform view of the Massey-Harris 101 Super Row-Crop illustrates the comfortable seat with a coil spring and a telescopic shock absorber. Massey-Harris was a leader in providing operator comfort already in the late 1930s. In comparing this innovative seat mounting to some of its contemporaries, some may be better, but others are no more than a pressed steel seat mounted wherever convenient, and with no spring mounting whatsoever!

A 1945 M-H catalog illustrates this 102GS Senior tractor from Massey-Harris. Gone was the boilerplate frame of the past, and in its place was a neat cast frame, attractive hood, and a radiator grille that emanated an automotive look. This model used a Continental Industrial engine with six cylinders of $3^5/_{16}$in bore and $4^3/_8$in stroke, yielding a displacement of 226 cubic inches. For drawbar work it was rated at 1500rpm, but for belt and road work the engine was rated at 1800rpm.

Massey-Harris 102GRC Senior Row-Crop tractors were essentially of the same design as the 102 standard-tread model. One of the innovative features was that the electric starter system came as standard equipment at the same time some of the competition was offering, and indeed recommending, the electric starter, yet it came as an extra-cost option. The power takeoff shaft and power lift system came as options on the 102GRC, however, even though many farmers had no need for this equipment in the 1940s.

The Massey-Harris 102 Junior standard-tread model was built from 1939 to 1946. A 102 Junior row-crop model was built during the same period. These tractors featured what was called Twin-Power. The idea was very simple: one engine speed was used for belt work, and a slower engine speed was used for tractive power. The two different speed levels were an innovative feature that helped to sell the tractor, but required virtually nothing in the way of additional manufacturing costs.

Built in 1945, this Massey-Harris 102GS Junior featured Twin-Power. When operating on the belt or the power takeoff shaft, the engine speed could be set to 1800rpm. For drawbar work, the setting was 1500rpm. The throttle lever came up to its first stop for the 1500rpm setting. By a simple hand movement, the first stop could be bypassed for the higher engine speed. The truth was that a great many of the Twin-Power tractors were run at the higher speed for drawbar work as well as on the belt pulley. This one is owned by Ivan Henderson of Cambridge, Ontario.

A front view of Ivan Henderson's 102GS Junior illustrates the unique radiator grille that more or less typified Massey-Harris tractors for several years, and through a number of different models. For some years, many of the M-H models were equipped with Continental Red Seal engines. However, Massey-Harris built all other major components of these tractors.

Chapter 2

Tractor Development of the 1940s and 1950s

In the opinion of many tractor collectors, the Massey-Harris "44" was one of the company's best tractors. Massey-Harris devotees often claim this model to be one of the best tractors ever built, regardless of make.

When the "44" first appeared in 1946, the company was already on the move, making the transition from war material to innovative tractor designs. Farmers were looking for a simple design, but a new emphasis was placed on increased horsepower and good fuel economy. Thus it was that Massey-Harris offered their tractors for use with gasoline, distillate, or propane fuels.

In addition, the company introduced the "44" Diesel model in 1948. For those farmers willing to pay the slightly higher list price for a diesel model, the reward came in excellent fuel economy and an extremely durable engine.

Such was the quality of the Massey-Harris line that essentially the same tractors were offered between 1946 and 1955. By that time, new technologies and recent changes in farming practices required new tractor models.

In 1951 Massey-Harris built nearly 20,000 copies of its Model 44 tractor at the Racine, Wisconsin, factory. The four-cylinder engine was rated at 1350rpm, and used a $3^7/_8$x$5^1/_2$in bore and stroke. In October 1947 this model was tested at Nebraska, where it delivered nearly 40 drawbar and almost 46 belt hp. A great many of these tractors are still in use, including this one owned by John Fisher of Milton, Ontario. The author has a 1953 model and, although unrestored, it is in excellent operating condition.

The MH-44 Standard-Tread was first built in 1946, followed a year later by the MH-44 Row-Crop. This catalog page from 1953 notes that the 44 was "Canada's most popular Tractor. . . ." Features included the Velvet Ride seat with its coil springing, hydraulic shock control, and swing-back feature. In 1948 the MH-44 Diesel Standard was introduced, followed the next year by the Diesel Row-Crop model. Production of the famous 44 series ended in 1955. This series was also built as propane models. Styles included the 44 Vineyard, 44 Orchard, 44 High-Arch Row-Crop, and 44 Single (front) Wheel Row-Crop.

MASSEY-HARRIS
3-plow 44-6

Massey-Harris offered the 44-6 row-crop tractor from 1947 to 1957. It was essentially the same as the 44 tractor, except that this model was equipped with a Continental F-226, six-cylinder engine. The 44-6 Standard-Tread was built in 1947, 1948, and 1950.

Apparently the six-cylinder design was provided for those farmers who preferred six-cylinder smoothness to the standard four-cylinder design. The author grew up around M-H tractors, and recalls seeing a couple of them in the neighborhood.

MH-44 tractors were tested at Nebraska three different times. The first test, No. 389, was conducted in 1947. In this instance, gasoline fuel was used. Test No. 426 of 1949 covered the MH-44 diesel model, and Test No. 427 had the Model 44 tractor burning distillate fuel.

The 44 models were enormously popular, especially in the gasoline version. Massey-Harris used their own four-cylinder diesel engine in the Model 44, which featured a Bosch injection system.

John Fisher of Milton, Ontario, owns this nicely restored MH-44 tractor. Production of this model began in 1946 for the standard-tread version, followed a year later by the row-crop model. In 1948 the famous MH-44 diesel made its first appearance, and was produced into 1955. The tractor's four-cylinder overhead-valve engine was designed and built by Massey-Harris.

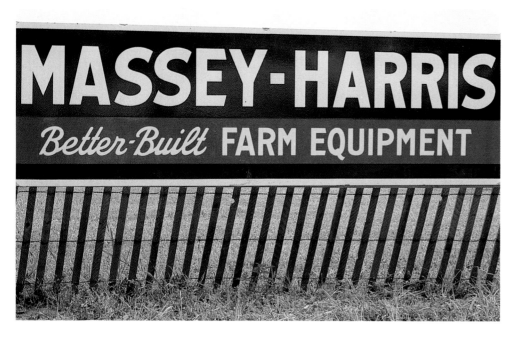

The black, red, and yellow Massey-Harris sign was familiar to farmers all over North America, as well as in many foreign countries. The company apparently exported large numbers of tractors and other equipment. Tractor demand in the years following World War II was unrelenting. Many farmers were prevented from buying new tractors during the Great Depression of the 1930s. As the decade of the 1940s opened, so did World War II, and this resulted in a temporary halt to virtually all new tractor production for several years. Thus, by 1946, many farmers had gone for fifteen years or more, using the same old relic every day.

Along with collectors of full-scale tractors, model makers constantly amaze tractor hobbyists. Here's a scale replica of an MH-44 tractor built from a garden tractor. This one was photographed at the Old Time Threshing & Antique Engine Show at Freeport, Illinois. Although model making has been a popular hobby in many countries, particularly in Great Britain, the hobby also has seen heavy activity in the United States within recent years.

Previous page
Here's a Massey-Harris 744 PD built in 1949 at the Kilmarnock Factory in Scotland. The P prefix stood for Perkins, since the Perkins six-cylinder P6 engine was used in these tractors. Its 288.6ci displacement yielded 46 belt hp. This example is owned by C. Smith of North Cadbury, and was photographed at the Great Dorset Steam Fair in Blandford, England, while belted to a thresher.

3-4 PLOW 44 SPECIAL

Takes 4-row equipment over long hours at low cost

The 44 Special is the tractor for the big farm . . . takes heavy implements through tough soil — over long, grueling hours . . . with power that stays on the pull and keeps ahead of your work.

You go right through the tough spots with a three or four bottom plow . . . slice through the clods of a rough field with a 15-foot disc . . . plant and cultivate with 4-row equipment . . . pull big combines, balers, choppers in heavy growth.

And you do it on less fuel. The 44 Special knows how to match fuel delivery to load demands . . . responds quickly when the pull gets heavy, eases you through on light loads.

277 cubic inch 4 cylinder engine, 5 forward speeds. Removable wet sleeves. Live P.T.O. 3-point, *Wrist-Action* Hitch-All. 45.85 drawbar horsepower, 50.29 on the belt.

Standard model for open field work

Single front wheel for narrow row crops

High arch front wheels for combination open field and row crop operations

MASSEY-HARRIS
2-3 plow 30

Previous page
Built from 1955 to 1957, the Model 44 Special was an upgrade of the earlier 44 tractor. The four-cylinder, 277ci engine delivered nearly 46 drawbar hp and slightly over 50 belt hp. Details of this model may be found in Nebraska Test No. 510. The earlier 44 gasoline model was tested under No. 389. A wide range of options was available, including standard-tread, high-arch front axle, and single-front-wheel types. The 44 Special was also available as a Special Cane model, listing at about $3,800. The regular row-crop style listed at approximately $3,200.

Between 1946 and 1952, Massey-Harris offered its popular 30 model. Advertised as a two- to three-plow model, it was equipped with a Continental four-cylinder engine with a $3^7/_{16}$x$4^3/_8$in bore and stroke. The L-head engine had a displacement of 162ci. This model listed at about $2,000. Details of its performance can be found under Nebraska Test No. 409. Massey-Harris offered a wide range of implements for the 30 that included a variety of cultivators built for virtually any crop or farming practice. Like other models of the period, the 30 was equipped with the Velvet Ride seat.

Production of the MH-22 tractors ran from 1948 to 1953. However, it appears that some of these tractors were sold as late as the 1954 model year. Rated at 1800rpm, this model featured a four-cylinder Continental engine with a 3³/₁₆x4³/₈in bore and stroke. Nebraska

Test 403 was run on this model in October 1948. The hydraulic system and power takeoff shaft came as standard equipment, but the pulley assembly added $40 to the list price of $1,725. This little tractor had a turning radius of only 7¹/₂ft.

Ivan Henderson of Cambridge, Ontario, is the proud owner of this Massey-Harris Model 22 standard-tread tractor. Of 1950 vintage, it carries Serial No. 3760. The Model 22 was tested at Nebraska in October of 1948; test results appear under No. 403. The 22 featured a Continental Red Seal engine. Rated at 1800rpm on the belt and 1500rpm on the drawbar, its four cylinders used a 3³/₁₆x4³/₈in bore and stroke. Bare weight of this tractor was 2,928lb.

Previous page
Model 22 tractors were available in row-crop and standard-tread versions. The rather scarce standard-tread model shown here is owned by Ivan Henderson of Cambridge, Ontario. In this tractor series, the model number indicates the company's horsepower rating for the model. In Nebraska Test No. 403 of 1948 the Model 22 delivered nearly 27 belt hp. Production of the Model 22 tractors ran from 1948 to 1952.

Production of the Model 33 tractors began in 1952 and ended in 1955. This encompassed all styles, including the 1953 Model 33 Diesel shown here. The Model 33 was offered in gasoline and diesel versions, with the latter style seeing rather limited production compared to its gasoline-powered partner. The diesel models delivered about 36 belt hp, slightly more than the 33 belt hp rating of the gas-powered models.

Model 33s were offered from 1952 to 1955. This tractor was a successor to the Model 30 built from 1947 to 1952. The 201ci engine put this tractor in the two- to three-plow class. Its four-cylinder engine featured slip-in sleeves, aluminum alloy pistons, and a one-piece manifold with individual cylinder porting. Along with the standard-tread design, 33 tractors could be furnished in a twin-wheel row-crop, single-wheel row-crop, and the high-arch designs. The block and upper crankcase were monocast for additional strength and stability. A 1953 catalog notes that the 33 could also be purchased on steel wheels.

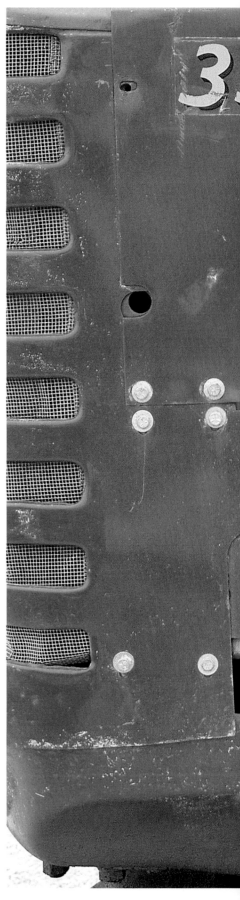

John Fisher of Milton, Ontario, owns this Massey-Harris Model 333 row-crop tractor. Built in 1956, it was a development of the earlier 33 model. Depth-O-Matic hydraulics and power steering were some of the available options. The 333 was built in tricycle, standard-tread, and high-arch configurations. Its last published retail price was $2,838 for the gasoline-powered row-crop model. The 333 series was built only in 1956 and 1957.

MH-333 gasoline-powered tractors used a Massey-Harris four-cylinder engine having a $3^{11}/_{16}$x$4^{7}/_{8}$in bore and stroke. Rated at 1500rpm, it had a 208ci displacement. The diesel version used a four-cylinder engine, again built by Massey-Harris, and carried the same bore and stroke for the same net displacement. However, the diesel version listed about $500 higher than the comparable gasoline model.

Built in 1956, John Hamilton's MH-333 tractor carries its owner home from the field. In addition to the hydraulic system and power steering, these models could also be furnished with an independent power takeoff shaft. Gasoline models could also be furnished for use with distillate or propane fuels. The earlier 33 models built from 1952 to 1956 used essentially the same four-cylinder engine, except that the bore was $3^5/_8$in. This was increased by $^1/_{16}$in for the 333.

Next page
Massey-Harris Colt models carried a four-cylinder engine with a displacement of 124ci. Of L-head design, it went so far as to feature valve rotators for maximum engine life and a minimum of service problems. In addition to a Standard-Tread model, the Colt was offered in the tricycle Row-Crop model shown here. The 1953 catalog also illustrates the high-arch extendable front axle, as well as the single-front-wheel design. Production of the Model 21 Colt was limited to 1952 and 1953.

MASSEY-HARRIS *Colt* AND *Mustang*

ROW CROP TRACTORS

The Colt and Mustang, with high arch extensible axle, have 21-inch clearance; adjusts in 4-inch steps from 60 to 88 inches.

The Colt and Mustang single front wheeler has a heavy steel yoke and axle; is designed for hard service.

Rear wheels adjust by reversing from 52 to 80 inches.

▶ **3 FRONT END DESIGNS AVAILABLE**

▶ **ADJUSTABLE REAR TREAD**

▶ **ADJUSTABLE 3-POINT HITCH AND SWINGING DRAWBAR**

Make a survey of the crops you grow, then select the Colt or Mustang Row Crop that meets your needs—the twin wheel model, the high arch front axle style or the single front wheeler. All these machines have a rear wheel adjustment from 52 to 80 inches. And with the exclusive Massey-Harris Depth-O-Matic follow-up hydraulic control, you merely touch a lever to raise and lower mounted implements. With no watching on your part, the hydraulic system maintains a constant depth.

This Model 11 Pony is owned by Vic Lauer of Mount Union, Iowa. Massey-Harris built the Pony between 1948 and 1957. The little Continental four-cylinder engine used a $2^3/_8$x$3^1/_2$in bore and stroke and, rated at 1800rpm, was capable of 10 drawbar and 11 belt hp. Built only as a standard-tread model, it listed at about $900. Options included a $68 belt pulley and power takeoff shaft, live power takeoff for $49, and a hand lift for implements at an additional $66.

In Nebraska Test No. 401 of 1948 the Massey-Harris Pony weighed in at 1,890lb. However, this little tractor delivered 1,432lb of maximum drawbar pull, or about 75 percent of its own weight. As with most other M-H models of the period, an Auto-Lite electrical system was standard equipment. The Continental four-cylinder engine was equipped with a Marvel-Schebler carburetor.

Bill Kuhn astride his 1949 Massey-Harris Pony. Industry records show that the Pony was offered during the 1948–57 model years. Tractors like the Pony were used for truck farming and other light work. Eventually, the industry built small tractors with much more power than the little 11hp engine of the Pony. Even more revolutionary, the gasoline engine was eventually replaced with a diesel, even in small tractors.

Previous page
This Massey-Harris Pony left the Woodstock Factory in Canada during 1949. It is owned by Bill Kuhn of Kinde, Michigan. The Pony badge should be on the nose of the hood, not on the side panels, but Kuhn likes them there! Small tractors like the Pony enjoyed brief popularity but were soon replaced in response to the cry for larger tractors. Eventually, the industry came full circle, and today's market offers a plethora of small tractors.

Model 23 Mustang tractors were built from 1952 to 1955. If the beginning serial numbers are a reasonable indicator of production, then the total run was likely under 3,500 copies. The Mustang carried a four-cylinder, 140ci engine. The Standard-Tread version listed at about $1,730, while the Row-Crop sold for approximately $1,880. It could be furnished with 11.00x28 or 12.00x28in rear tires. Disc brakes were standard equipment, along with worm-and-sector steering, push-button starting, and an adjustable drawbar. An adjustable three-point hitch was optional.

Sold between 1954 and 1957, the Model 16 Pacer was available in the standard-tread style shown here. Thus equipped, it sold at about $1,400. This price included the belt pulley and power takeoff shaft—adding the independent shaft was a $50 option. The Pacer was furnished with a Continental four-cylinder engine having a $2^7/_8$x$3^1/_2$in bore and stroke for a 91ci displacement. The front and rear treads were adjustable for various row crops, and the belly clearance of $20^1/_2$in permitted work in established fields.

"The biggest farm Tractor on wheels. . . ." Thus stated a 1953 M-H catalog in reference to the Model 55 tractor. Production of the 55 gasoline model began in 1946, followed three years later by the MH-55 Diesel. Built only as a standard-tread model, the 55 was also available for use with propane fuel. For western farmers, Massey-Harris offered the 55 in a special Western Model with 18.00x26in rear tires. A rear extension was added to the platform to enable operating the tractor from a standing position. An over-center hand clutch was also standard equipment for this model. Riceland and Hillside models were built from 1949 to 1955. Production of the MH-55 ended for all variants in 1955.

Offered for 1956–57, the MH-333 was the beginning of the end for this tractor style. During the same period, the company also offered the Massey-Ferguson 35, 50, and 65 tractors. The 333 was available in gasoline and diesel models. The gasoline version yielded 37 belt hp, while the diesel model displayed about 42hp. Details of these two models are found in Nebraska Test Numbers 577 and 603, respectively. The 333 was offered in tricycle, standard-tread, and high-arch models.

MASSEY-HARRIS   THE BIG MASTER OF 4-PLOW FARMING

Massey-Harris built the 444 tractor from 1956 to 1958. Like the smaller 333, it was offered in gasoline and diesel versions; the gasoline style could be modified to burn propane fuel as well. Calling it "The big master of 4-plow farming," M-H continued using their 277ci, four-cylinder engine developed some years before. Both the 333 and 444 featured a ten-speed transmission. An independent power takeoff shaft came as standard equipment, but power steering cost extra.

Next page
Like most competing manufacturers, Massey-Harris offered many of their tractor models in an LP-gas version. This fuel gained considerable popularity in the 1950s, and remained as a viable option until diesel engines became standard equipment for farm tractors. Shown here are the Model 444 and 555 LP-gas versions of 1956. Except for the necessary changes required for fuel equipment, the only other change was to slightly alter the compression ratio for the most efficient use of this fuel. The 333 tractor was also built in an LP-gas version.

NEW 444 L. P.

Full 4 plow power—277 cubic inch engine with 8.7 to 1 compression ratio—Depth-o-matic hydraulic system—10 forward speeds, 2 reverse—3-Point Hitch-All—Standard, High-Arch, Row Crop and Single Front Wheel models.

NEW 555 L. P.

Husky 5 plow power—382 cubic inch engine with 8.57 to 1 compression ratio—hydraulics available—4 forward speeds and reverse—Standard, Riceland and Western models. Foot or hand clutch.

MASSEY-HARRIS

555

FIVE-PLOW POWER AT ITS GREATEST

The toughest tractor on four wheels, with a mighty 382 cu. in. engine and 60½ drawbar horsepower. Plows 3½ to 4 acres an hour or stubble-mulches up to 75 acres a day.

A big 382ci engine was featured in the MH-555 gasoline model. Offered in the 1955–58 period, this was one of the largest farm tractors of its time. Power steering was standard equipment, and like the 333 and 444, the big 555 featured a 12-volt electrical system. The transition from 6 to 12 volts took place over several years, but was of major benefit to the industry. Massey-Harris advertised their later models as having Cyclo-Head Combustion. This was simply a cylinder head and piston design intended to squeeze every bit of power from every drop of fuel.

A front view of the MH-745 tractor illustrates its distinctive radiator grille. The 745 was built at the Kilmarnock Factory in Scotland, and this particular tractor emerged in 1954. About 11,000 of the Model 745s were built at Kilmarnock over a four-year period.

Next page

This nicely restored MH-745 tractor is owned by Barry Tuck from Wareham, England. It was photographed at the Great Dorset Steam Fair. The 745 was powered by a Perkins L4 diesel engine. Massey-Harris used Perkins engines in selected models over many years.

In a 1958 catalog, Massey-Ferguson called the Ferguson 35 the "world's most copied tractor." The three-point hitch system added new flexibility to field work, promoting efficiency and reducing operator fatigue. Another innovative feature was the tractormeter which helped select the correct ground speed and engine rpm to suit a specific task. Thousands of these tractors were equipped with aftermarket loaders, and this truly made the Ferguson 35 one of the most useful tractors of its time.

Chapter 3

Massey-Ferguson Tractors

Since various books have already alluded to the Ford and Ferguson partnership, this study has concentrated on the tractors using the Ferguson system, rather than the financial details of the arrangement. It is significant, however, that Henry Ford was highly impressed with Harry Ferguson's three-point hitch system. In fact, Ford was so impressed that he obtained manufacturing rights to the Ferguson system, doing so on the basis of a handshake. All went fairly well for several years, despite what might be described as the volatile personalities of both men.

Eventually, the agreement ended, and Ferguson sought to go it alone in the tractor business. After 4½ years of litigation, Ford and Ferguson finally made a settlement.

However, in only a few months' time, Ferguson was in serious financial troubles. So, in 1953 the Massey-Harris and Ferguson organizations merged to form Massey-Harris-Ferguson Limited. This was later abbreviated to Massey-Ferguson.

As of the early 1970s, Massey-Ferguson products were being built in eighty-seven factories in thirty countries. Half of these were developing nations. Of its products, 93 percent were being sold in 190 countries outside of Canada.

The dramatic changes in the farm economy over the past two decades have changed this picture considerably. Like all farm machinery builders, Massey-Ferguson has undergone its share of factory closings and belt tightening in recent years.

Now . . . the high-profit

advantages of both

DIESEL POWER

and Ferguson System

Ferguson Model 35 tractors were also available in a diesel version. This model was built concurrently with the Ferguson 35 gasoline model—that is, from 1955 to 1957. The four-cylinder engine used a 3⁵/₁₆x4in bore and stroke for a displacement of 137.8ci, and had a compression ratio of 20:1. This engine featured the Ricardo Comet combustion system. Rated at 32.7 drawbar hp, it was capable of pulling a three-bottom mounted plow in most soils. Extra-large truck-type brakes were a standard feature. An overload release on the three-point hitch system prevented damage to the tractor and implement by cutting traction if an obstruction was hit.

Between 1958 and 1964 Massey-Ferguson built the MF-65 tractor. Like the MF-50 and the Ferguson 35, it featured 4-Way Work Control. This concept included Quadramatic Control for more accurate operation, Dual-Range Transmission for greater flexibility, Variable-Drive PTO (power takeoff) for synchronized power, and Two-Stage Clutching—the latter requiring only one pedal for transmission and power takeoff shaft. MF-65 tractors were offered in gasoline, LP-gas, and diesel versions. Nebraska Test No. 659 on the gasoline model indicates about 43 belt hp; this model carried a Continental four-cylinder, 176ci engine. The MF-65 diesel used a Perkins four-cylinder engine with a 3.6x5.0in bore and stroke. In Test No. 745 it yielded 48.59 power takeoff hp. Test No. 808 was run on this same basic model, except that in this case the compression ratio was raised to 17.5, compared to 17.4 in the earlier test. The second test disclosed 50.98 power takeoff hp.

You can easily see where you're going, get a full view of your work with this front-mounted cultivator. No need to twist and strain to see what you've done. In addition to full, unobstructed vision, you get the additional advantages of Hydramic Control. Depth of cultivation is accurately controlled with the MH 50's revolutionary hydraulic system.

Attached to a rigid tool bar mounted behind the front axle, cultivators handle two rows spaced 28 to 42 inches apart. Available with either spring trip shanks or spring teeth. Six spring trip shanks or spring teeth are mid-mounted on four gangs individually supported by heavy 1¾ inch square tool bars. Five spring trip shanks or seven spring teeth are mounted on the rear 1¾ inch square tool bar.

MH 122 2-ROW CULTIVATOR

Front-Mounted . . .

All-Around Vision . . .

Hydramic Power

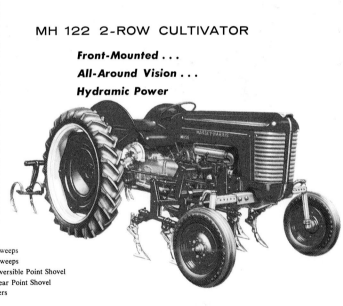

Available Equipment

Spring Trip Shanks	12-inch Sweeps
Spring Teeth	16-inch Sweeps
6-inch Sweeps	3-inch Reversible Point Shovel
8-inch Sweeps	5-inch Spear Point Shovel
8-inch Sweep right and left half sweeps	Disc Hillers
10-inch Sweeps	Shields

The MH-50 tractor first saw light in 1956. It reflected the changeover to a low-profile design, similar to that of the Ferguson tractors. A major design feature was the integral three-point hitch system that would revolutionize farm implement design. Shown here is an MH-50 tractor with the MH-122 mounted cultivator. The low-profile design permitted unobstructed visibility, and the Hydramic depth control accurately maintained the selected operating depth. Massey-Ferguson Model 50 tractors continued from 1958 to 1964.

When it was introduced in 1959, the MF-85 was the first and only five-plow tractor to be equipped with the Ferguson system. Wrist-action links and independently hinged lift arms provided new operator convenience. The top links were fully adjustable to properly level implements when in their working position. A four-piston, Scotch yoke hydraulic pump provided a capacity of 7gpm, and a two-stage air cleaner, plus an oil-to-air intercooler came as standard equipment. During its 1959–62 production run, the MF-85 was available in gasoline or LP-gas versions, along with a diesel model. Standard-tread, tricycle, and high-arch models were available with any of the three fuel choices.

REAL LUGGING POWER

FOR PULL-TYPE

IMPLEMENTS

Built from 1959 to 1962, the big MF-88 tractor was available with a gasoline or a diesel engine. The diesel's 276.5ci displacement was yielded by a Continental four-cylinder engine having a 4x5½in bore and stroke. In Nebraska Test No. 765 it yielded a maximum of 63.31 power takeoff hp. Power steering was standard equipment, as was the dual-range transmission with eight forward and two reverse speeds. A rear-mounted belt pulley was optional, but the double-disc brakes were standard equipment for this tractor.

Introduced in 1964, the MF-175 tractor was offered in gasoline and diesel versions. It is shown here with a Massey-Ferguson mounted plow. M-F offered their mounted plows in several distinct models, with numerous attachments and enhancements available for each model. The gasoline and diesel models both used a Perkins four-cylinder engine having a 3⁷/₈x5in bore and stroke. Both were rated at 2200rpm, and both developed approximately 63 power takeoff hp. Production of the 175 tractor continued into 1975.

The MF-290 tractor built from 1983 to 1986 was a low-profile model that could be furnished with an eight-speed manual transmission or the twelve-speed Multi-Power transmission. The 290 could also be furnished with a standard clearance or a high-clearance chassis. A Perkins AD4.248 engine was standard equipment. This direct-injection diesel was capable of 65 power takeoff hp at 2200rpm. The rear axles were of the outboard planetary flanged design, and featured a differential lock.

A Perkins AD4.236 four-cylinder engine was featured in the MF-670 tractor. This model was capable of 55 power takeoff hp. Built in the 1983–86 time frame, the 670 was equipped with a twelve-speed synchromesh transmission. Hydrostatic power steering came as standard equipment, along with an advanced Ferguson full-range hydraulic system. A Category II, three-point hitch also was standard equipment with this model. It used the wrist-action links pioneered by Ferguson many years before.

Built during 1983–84, the MF-698 was a top-of-the-line tractor at the time. This model was capable of 78 power takeoff hp, and was billed as being the "ultimate luxury tractor in this size range." In addition to the cab model shown here, the 698 was also available in a platform model for those who did not desire or need year-round weather protection. The twelve-speed gearbox gave a speed range of 1.2 to 15.4mph. Syncromesh couplers on second, third, fifth, and sixth gears provided effortless changes on-the-go.

Massey-Harris entered the engine business through the buyout of Deyo-Macey Engine Co. at Binghamton, New York. Deyo-Macey had developed a line of gas engines by 1905, and these were made available in sizes ranging from 1½ to 16hp. M-H moved the Deyo-Macey factory equipment to its Weston, Ontario, plant and continued building gasoline engines for several years. As indicated in this catalog illustration, the M-H engine line ranged from 1½ to 20hp.

Massey-Harris offered gasoline engines as late as 1945. The original M-H engines built at the Weston Plant had long since disappeared from production. Subsequently, it appears that M-H offered engines that were actually built by other manufacturers. Such was the case with this series of engines offered in the 1945 M-H catalog. The engines were, in fact, built by Cushman Motor Works at Lincoln, Nebraska.

MASSEY-HARRIS ENGINES
2, 3 AND 4 H.P. VARIABLE SPEED

The popularity of the MF-300 combine is evidenced by its long production run from 1968 to 1978. This big machine could be equipped with a Perkins AD4.203 diesel engine or a Chrysler H225 gasoline engine. Both were capable of over 70hp. This series also featured MF Quick-Attach corn heads and grain tables. Advertising of the period indicates that headers could be switched in "five minutes or less with a little practice." The full-comfort cab kept the operator away from dust, dirt, and bad weather. Standard equipment included a cab air filter and pressurizing fan. Air conditioning was optional.

Chapter 4

Beyond Tractors: Combines and Implements

During the 1946-55 period, Massey-Harris also spent considerable sums in tuning their combines and adding new machines to the line. Massey-Harris developed the concept of the self-propelled combine in the 1930s. From the days of the "Harvest Brigade" the Massey-Harris combines evolved into some of the finest in the industry. Since Massey-Harris was a multinational company, many thousands of their combines and tractors were exported to all major grain-producing areas of the world.

Initially, the self-propelled combine was well received in the large grain-growing areas of the United States, Canada, and other major grain-producing countries. The average "quarter-section" farmer (160 acres), was content to use a much smaller pull-type combine, and Massey-Harris offered many different sizes and styles of its "Clipper" series. As farming continued to move toward fewer farmers and larger acre-

ages, the self-propelled combine gained favor, even on smaller-sized farms. In recent years the combine market has offered virtually nothing except self-propelled models.

Probably one of the most innovative developments of the period was the Massey-Harris self-propelled corn picker. This interesting machine was marketed for only a few years; by then, farmers were changing over to the corn combine in place of the time-honored corn picker. Only twenty years earlier, the majority of ear corn was picked by hand. With the development of successful (and accepted) corn picker designs in the 1930s, the harvest of the corn crop was finally mechanized. Yet, the introduction of the corn combine in the 1950s would relegate the corn picker to obsolescence within another twenty years. Today, a relatively small amount of corn is harvested in the ear . . . the majority is harvested with the corn combine. Who can predict the changes ahead?

MASSEY-HARRIS NEW No. 5 BINDER.

Although the International Harvester Company and other US manufacturers were dominant in the US market, Massey-Harris held a major position in Canada, as well as in many foreign countries. The M-H No. 5 grain binder was one of many different farm implements that were widely sold in the international market. Roller bearings were extensively used. An undated Massey-Harris catalog also notes that "bearings for platform rollers are of hard maple soaked in boiling tallow." Although surprising to many, hard maple wooden bearings could run for years with very little attention except for regular greasing.

Next page
One of the most unique Massey-Harris machines was the self-propelled corn picker, introduced in 1948 and built for about ten years. M-H claimed that this machine had the biggest capacity of anything in the field. It did, in fact, have a ten-roll husking bed, which was substantially larger than most of the competing models. M-H equipped the machine with the Continental F-226 engine to handle the picker and the load under all conditions. Extra equipment included vine knives, wheel weights, rubber husking rolls, and special tires. The two-row mounted picker was offered from 1952 to 1958.

MASSEY-HARRIS *Self-Propelled* CORN PICKER

New MOUNTED PICKER . . . takes but a few

minutes to attach and detach . . .

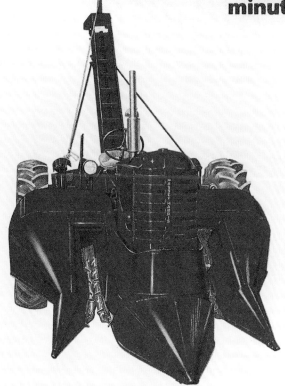

Here's capacity, correct weight distribution, complete visibility, ease of attaching and low investment cost in a 2-row mounted corn harvester.

You drive right into the Massey-Harris mounted picker . . . special mounting skids guide the picking unit saddles into place on the main drive shaft quickly and accurately. The shaft runs under the tractor and forms a hinge point on which the entire unit pivots when the snouts are raised or lowered. You use tractor power in making the hook-up . . . eliminating heavy lifting. The Massey-Harris Picker is built low for complete visibility and comfort. And the majority of weight is distributed over the tractor axle resulting in easier handling and better traction. Snouts and center divider are full floating . . . follow the land to get down stalks. Snapping rolls are 39 inches long and the inner roll is inclined to lay the ears on the leading edge of the husking bed. 45-inch husking rolls clean the corn thoroughly. Rubber paddles move the corn over the rolls and deliver it to the large hopper and wagon elevator. Picker mechanism is driven from the belt pulley shaft. The entire Picker weighs only 1650 pounds, yet is built with an extra margin of strength to take the tough conditions of the corn harvest.

A HIGH QUALITY SEPARATOR AT SPECIAL VALUE PRICES

MASSEY-HARRIS
No. 9
CREAM SEPARATOR

CLOSE SKIMMING—The No. 9 has the Massey-Harris close skimming bowl with 6-point film flow distribution which spreads the milk over the discs in a thin film giving close skimming. This kind of separation brings you more money from your dairy herd.

EASY TO FILL—Supply can is held firm—no tipping when you pour milk into it. High quality tinware is easy to clean and gives long wear.

EASY TO TURN—Simple gearing, well made of high quality materials and efficient oiling system give smooth-running and easy turning. Every machine is run at the factory for several hours.

DEPENDABLE SERVICE — Users of Massey-Harris products appreciate the prompt, efficient service available to them through the company's branch and dealer organization. It saves time and money to be able to get prompt service.

SPECIAL low prices give you the most value for the money—order from your local Massey-Harris dealer.

$60.25	$71.50	$83.50
400-450 lbs.	550-600 lbs.	850-900 lbs.

Moncton (Freight prepaid)

The 1945 Massey-Harris catalog included cream separators as a part of the product line. This No. 9 separator was available in three different sizes. The smallest could handle 400 to 450lb of milk per hour and sold for $60.25.

The largest had a capacity of 850 to 900lb of milk per hour and retailed at $83.50. Note that the No. 9 is cranked by hand; perhaps there were other models that could be equipped with an electric motor.

From binders to wagons, the Massey-Harris line also included grain grinders and hammer mills. For 1945 the company was offering the No. 11 tractor grinder, a 10½ burr mill designed especially for tractor use. In addition, M-H offered the smaller No. 12 grinder which could be equipped with an electric motor or a gas engine. The No. 12 could be furnished with the choice of motors in 1½, 2, or 3hp, or the customer could mount his own motor or engine to this grinder.

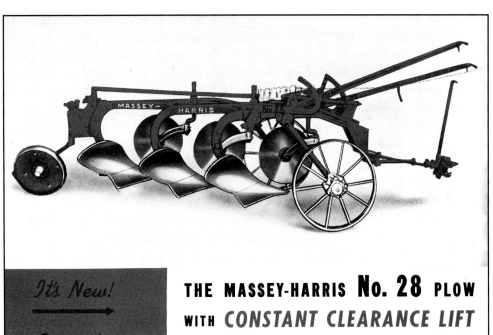

For some years, Massey-Harris produced the No. 28 tractor plow. In fact, M-H was a well-known plow builder, especially after acquiring Verity Plow Co. and other concerns. The No. 28 featured the Constant Clearance Lift, an M-H exclusive. It permitted a full 7½in clearance regardless of the plowing depth. Whether plowing 3in deep or 12in deep, this plow always maintained a 7½in clearance when out of the ground. Other exclusive features were the use of adjustable chilled iron wheel bearings, plus its double-X frame bracing.

M-H one-way disc plows were offered in many different styles and sizes. This model of the 1950s featured the M-H Roto-Lift system which rolled the discs out of the ground in only 24in of forward travel. In less than 40in of forward travel, lifting was completed to full clearance. Some models could be equipped with an all-steel grain box to permit discing and seeding in one pass. While this unit uses a mechanical lift system, hydraulic power would soon become standard equipment.

It's New! → Saves time → Saves power →

THE MASSEY-HARRIS No. 28 PLOW
WITH CONSTANT CLEARANCE LIFT

New farming methods and increased plowing speeds require faster, lighter-draft plows for most efficient operation. Older type plows with quick-turn moldboards drain the power and slow up the speed of your tractor—resulting in high fuel costs and considerable loss of time.

To the thousands of cost-wise farmers who have been waiting for a really *new* kind of plow for today's new conditions, Massey-Harris proudly presents the new No. 28 with *Constant Clearance Lift!* Here's the plow that's revolutionary . . . a real contribution to better plowing. Three new *exclusive* features plus a dozen other practical plow improvements put the new No. 28 in a class by itself. Let's take them in order and find out *why* the No. 28 gives you the *most* plow for your money.

New MASSEY-HARRIS no.2

For Massey-Harris Colt and Mustang Tractors

Handle more than 50 jobs the year 'round on your farm with the new Massey-Harris No. 2 Hydraulic Loader. And you'll do the work with less effort, too, because the No. 2 is available with a hydraulic dumping unit. A touch of the handy lever trips the bucket at any height you desire. Another touch of the lever and the bucket re-positions itself *under power*. There's no danger of accidental dumping, no return springs to get out of adjustment . . . you have positive, complete control at all times.

Husky Construction Means Extra Strength, Longer Life

Booms are of sturdy 2-inch steel pipe construction, cross-braced for extra rigidity. Big 3-inch diameter rams have a stroke of 15 inches . . . raise loads to a height of 8 feet.

In order to maximize the potential uses for the M-H Colt and Mustang tractors, Massey-Harris offered their No. 2 loader. It was designed especially for use with these models. Dual hydraulic controls actuated the lift and dump cylinders. In addition, a handy control lever on the Colt and Mustang two-way cylinder permitted the operation of a rear-mounted scraper or other tool, with total independence from the loader hydraulics.

M-H topped off their hydraulic loader line with the big No. 10 model. The MH-50 tractor, as shown here, featured a lift of 8½ft and a maximum lifting load of 1,500lb. The No. 10 used a mechanically operated bucket which, when tripped with a rope, would latch itself when dumping its load. Big 3¼in cylinder rams also were used, and the unit was carried on massive 4in steel mounting brackets.

Another M-H design of the 1950s was this MH-20 self-propelled swather. It could mow, rake, and spray—triple duty from a single machine. The lever-type steering control was precise, yet permitted "turning on a dime." The table and reel were hydraulically controlled for an infinitely variable cutting height anywhere from 2 to 20in. Swathing speeds were infinitely variable, anywhere from a crawl up to 5mph.

 **MASSEY-HARRIS**

RUST COTTON PICKER

MOST PRACTICAL APPROACH TO MECHANICAL PICKING

MODEL M COTTON PICKER . . . picks 36 to 42-inch rows . . . easily attached, detached . . . one picking unit . . . 3 M.P.H. picking speed . . . short turning radius . . . 600-800-lb. basket capacity . . . hydraulic dump. Fits 33, 44, 44 Special, 333 and 444 row crop tractors.

PICKING UNITS — both front and rear have 1280 picking fingers each — more than in any other single row picker. It means greater picking ability, more capacity, cleaner operation.

All steel frame is built to take the twists and jars of rough ground travel — holds operating units in perfect alignment.

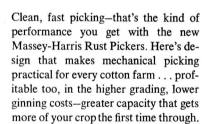

Clean, fast picking—that's the kind of performance you get with the new Massey-Harris Rust Pickers. Here's design that makes mechanical picking practical for every cotton farm . . . profitable too, in the higher grading, lower ginning costs—greater capacity that gets more of your crop the first time through.

Smooth, non-aggressive picking fingers pick completely through the plant —select only the open bolls. There's no roping of the cotton—no staining, less trash.

Simplified design lets you operate in the normal forward position—makes adjustments easily. Sturdy, balanced construction—easy-on, easy-off mounting. Hydraulic controls.

MODEL MT COTTON PICKER . . . tandem picking units . . . picks 36 to 42-inch rows . . . covers 1 acre per hour . . . no conversion kits or tractor changes . . . quick mounting. Easy to demount. Fits 44, 44 Special and 444 row crop tractors.

LOW COST PICKING FINGERS are smooth, non-aggressive in action. Each is mounted individually in removable slots. Low in cost — easy to replace.

Previous page
Although our present research has not determined the full extent of the Massey-Harris cotton picker line, there is no doubt about these machines of the 1950s. As is well known, cotton picking was one of the last major crop jobs to be mechanized. Like the corn picker, which also defied practicality for many years, the cotton picker went through decades of trials and experiments before successful harvesting methods were developed. These machines could be fitted over the Model 33, 44, 44 Special, 333, and 444 row-crop tractors.

Massey-Harris offered an extensive line of grain drills. While still retaining the steel-wheeled drills of earlier years, the 1956 M-H line included the No. 26 grain and fertilizer drill shown here. It permitted drilling and fertilizing in one

pass. The low-profile design permitted easier loading, and the all-steel construction reduced weight while increasing strength. Two sizes were available: thirteen or fifteen runs, on a 7in spacing, and single or double disc.

Dating from the mid-1950s, this Massey-Harris Slicer Baler is shown with its own engine drive. At this time, M-H balers could be furnished with a power takeoff drive or with a Wisconsin air-cooled engine. This model featured a 52in pickup to handle large, fluffy windrows. An auger feed carried the crop to the wadboard and plunger. Extensive use was made of sealed ball bearings. Permanently sealed bearings began making their appearance in the early 1950s and although this innovation met with cautious approval by farmers initially, subsequent improvements and a longer running life brought the sealed bearing to full acceptance.

Building tractors was a major activity for the Massey-Harris factories by the early 1930s. With the advent of row-crop tractors came the need for implements designed especially for use with the row-crop designs. One of the most important implements was the cultivator and M-H offered extensive varieties of these implements. The cultivators were not only tailored to specific tractor models, but were also designed for specific crop needs and farming practices. A 1953 Massey-Harris catalog illustrates the No. 20 beet and bean cultivator mounted on a Colt tractor.

THIS IS THE COMBINE THAT MAKES HARVESTING EASIER, QUICKER, AND CHEAPER

A GREAT HELP WHERE THERE IS A SHORTAGE OF LABOR

A truly one-man combine—on many farms 'teen age young-sters operate the Massey-Harris self-propelled. It is easy to steer—anyone who can drive a motor car can easily learn to run a No. 21.

A REAL GRAIN SAVER

Opens up the field, and works close to roads, fences, or ditches without knocking down any of the standing crop. Has the capacity to do a good clean job in heavy yields, down, tangled, grain, etc. Unexcelled for harvesting seed crops with minimum loss through shelling.

SPEEDY, LOW-COST HARVESTING

Labor and operating costs are low with a Massey-Harris self-propelled. One man does the operating—one motor supplies the power to propel the machine and work the mechanism. With its large capacity the Massey-Harris gets over a large acreage in a day giving full advantage of favorable weather.

SPECIAL FEATURES DEVELOPED BY MASSEY-HARRIS FOR COMBINE HARVESTERS

The self-propelled combine perfected by Massey-Harris engineers has bar type cylinder, recleaner type shaker shoe, patented elevator to cylinder and other features developed by Massey-Harris in its long experience of building combines famous for their outstanding harvesting ability.

Massey-Harris pioneered the self-propelled combine. The Model 21 appeared in the early 1940s and in 1948 had a list price of $3,494. Massey-Harris had developed an enviable reputation with their pull-type combines, and building the self-propelled machine helped to revolutionize grain harvesting. For one thing, the combine ended a century of threshing machine use as it evolved from a crude chaff piler to the all-steel machine with roller bearings. For another, the combine, and particularly the self-propelled model, dramatically reduced the extra labor needed for grain harvesting.

Massey-Harris introduced the No. 15 combine in the late 1930s. It could be purchased in either a 6ft or an 8ft version. Designed as a one-man machine, it featured easy changing of the cylinder speed for harvesting various crops. This was achieved through changing roller chain sprockets on the cylinder drive. Massey-Harris gained early experience in the combine business, and had gained earlier status with its grain binders, threshers, and other harvesting equipment.

Next page
Massey-Harris offered the Super 26 and Super 27 combine models in the early 1950s. Both models used a Chrysler Industrial engine, and the multiple-speed drive system permitted up to thirty-two controlled forward speeds. These ranged from a crawl up to a maximum of 7½mph. The drive consisted of variable-pitch V-belt pulleys and a simple two-speed transmission. A toggle switch next to the steering wheel provided electric control for raising and lowering the grain table. These machines could also be equipped with track-laying equipment for rice harvesting. The Super 27 listed at about $5,100.

Balanced Separation is yours

ONLY IN THESE FIELD-PROVEN MASSEY-HARRIS COMBINES

the big capacity Super 26

With its 12-foot table and Balanced Separation, the big-capacity Super 26 cuts its way through 50 acres of grain a day . . . more economically than you ever thought possible. Balanced Separation, with its more efficient cylinder, longer straw walkers and more efficient cleaning areas, separates whatever you cut. Straw is kept loose . . . open . . . always moving . . . so all of the grain falls through. And it's cleaner grain . . . directional wind control does a thorough job of removing chaff.

There is balanced design in the combine itself . . . a low center of gravity makes for easier steering, easier handling, comfortable, safe operation.

**Available in 12 and 10-foot widths.
(Tank or Bagger type as ordered)**

and Super 27

You get more capacity with the Super 27 . . . more speed, convenience, visibility, comfort—more of everything that makes harvesting simpler, easier, faster, more profitable. You cut more acres a day with the 16-foot 27 . . . getting more grain, cleaner grain because of Balanced Separation. It's controlled separation . . . every step of the way. Balanced Separation is exclusively Massey-Harris . . . the result of more than 50 years' experience in building better combines.

Available in 16, 14, and 12-foot cuts. Tank machines (as shown) or Bagger type.

the biggest capacity combine on wheels

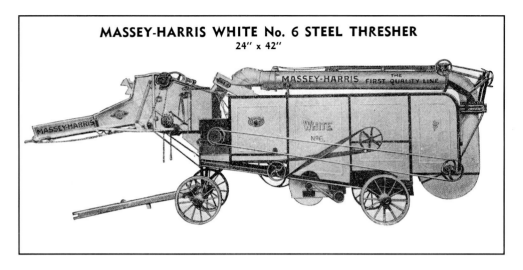

MASSEY-HARRIS WHITE No. 6 STEEL THRESHER
24" x 42"

A 1945 Massey-Harris catalog illustrates the No. 6 steel thresher. This model featured welded-frame construction to reduce bulk and weight. Fully equipped, it weighed only 4,000lb. The nine-bar cylinder had a width of 24in and operated at 1200rpm. The separator was 42in wide and included full-width straw racks with a total length of 10ft. Despite the quality of this machine, combines were displacing the time-honored thresher. By the time 1950 rolled around, very few companies were still building threshing machines.

Next page
Massey-Harris offered the Model 80 and Model 90 combines from 1953 to 1956. Both models used a six-cylinder Chrysler Industrial engine; the Model 80 used a 230ci size, but the Model 90 featured a 250ci. Both models used four straw walkers of full-cylinder width. While the Model 80 could be fitted with 10, 12, or 14ft grain tables, the range of the Model 90 was 12, 14, or 16ft. Extra cylinder sprockets were available to provide cylinder speeds ranging from 230 to 1190rpm. With a 14ft grain table, the Model 90 listed at about $6,250.

During the mid-1950s, Massey-Harris introduced their Clipper 50 Corn Combine. This tractor-powered machine permitted harvesting of small grains and corn with nothing more than a change of heads and some simple adjustments. An extension axle unit moved the right-hand wheel outward to conform with standard row spacings. Despite its advantages, the pull-type corn combine never achieved great popularity—this had already been usurped by the self-propelled combine.

UNMATCHED

. GRAIN-SAVING DESIGN

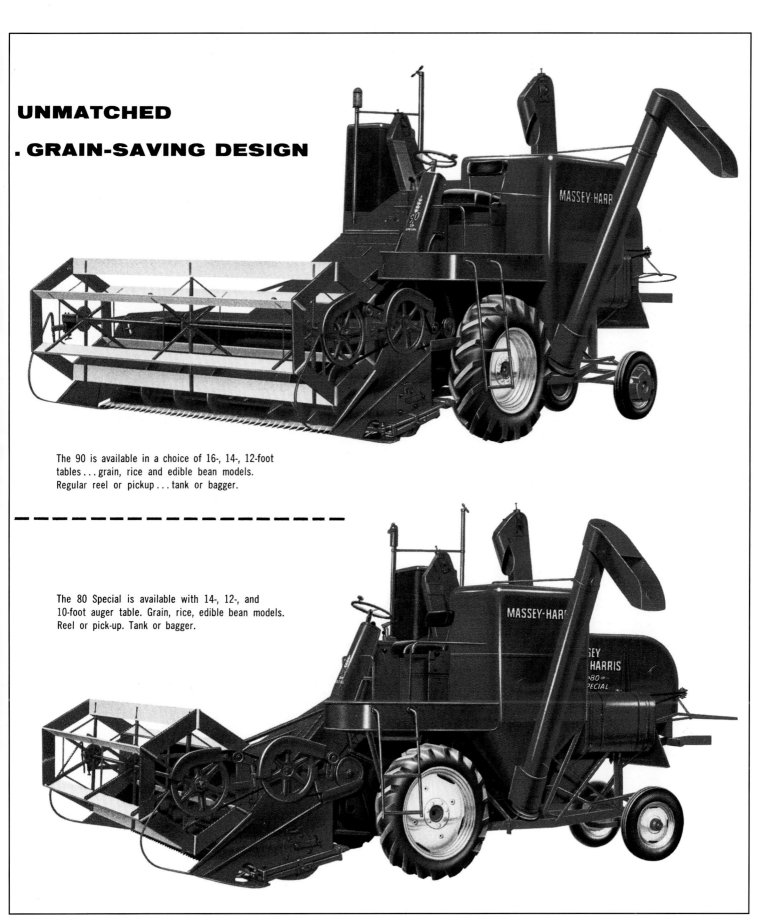

The 90 is available in a choice of 16-, 14-, 12-foot tables...grain, rice and edible bean models. Regular reel or pickup...tank or bagger.

The 80 Special is available with 14-, 12-, and 10-foot auger table. Grain, rice, edible bean models. Reel or pick-up. Tank or bagger.

90 AND 80 SELF-PROPELLED EDIBLE BEAN COMBINES . . . enclosed gear drive, variable speed, hydraulic controls. 90 has 37-inch cylinder — 80 has 32-inch. Equipped with cutter-bar and reel. Pick-up is extra equipment.

CLIPPER 50 PEANUT COMBINE

20

Previous page
During the mid-1950s Massey-Harris offered the Model 80 and Model 90 combines in a special Edible Bean version. It was designed with a special spike-toothed cylinder and open concave. The cylinder speed was very low compared to ordinary grain machines, and with the open concave, threshed beans dropped directly onto the grain pan. In all, M-H offered seven different combine models for this specialized duty during the general time frame. Also available was the Clipper 50 Peanut Combine, a specialized machine with a capacity of up to twenty acres per day. Other specialized machines were designed for flax and other types of seeds and grasses.

The MF-72 combine was available in a pull-type model, as well as in a self-propelled version. Production of these machines ran from 1959 to 1966. The pull-type machine was ordinarily supplied with an 8ft cut, but a 10ft table was also available. In addition, this machine could be equipped with its own engine in lieu of the regular power

takeoff drive. Model 72 self-propelled combines could be purchased with a 10ft or a 12ft grain table. It could also be purchased as the MF-72 Soybean Special, and could be equipped with the MF-22 corn head. The Chrysler Industrial engine developed 57hp; it was of L-head design and had a displacement of 230.2ci.

Index